Another 4 Years?

Another 4 Years?

Recognizing President Barack Obama's Accomplishments

Emily Gaddi
Master of Arts in Management

To order additional copies of this book, contact:
Xlibris Corporation
1-888-795-4274
www.Xlibris.com
Orders@Xlibris.com
120747

CONTENTS

Washington, D.C. is unique amongAmerican cities because it was established by the Constitution of the United States to serve as the nation's capital. From the beginning it has been embroiled in political maneuvering, sectional conflicts, issues of race, national identity, compromise, and of course, power (Washington.org/about-washington-dc). It is a very interesting and captivating city to visit. My impression was that, you have to be a very well educated and a fully equipped person to be a part of D.C. Is it a very competitive, aggressive, and ambitious city? Definitely! I did not find it very appealing when I was younger because I was not into politics. I am not a lawyer, and it was not my kind of city because my forte has been in retailing. I am more of a New York type of person. The trip to visit Washington, D.C. was very satisfying for me in several ways. It gave me the opportunity to see the beauty and sophistication of the architecture of the city and to appreciate the excellent planning of those who started the city. As an adult rather than a child during this visit, I also learned to appreciate the dynamic nature of the people who work in Washington.

At any rate, I fell in love with D.C. during my visit because it has a lot of things to offer for an aspiring doctoral candidate like me. I know, I have a future in the city and I will take all the necessary opportunities that come to visit it again. I found it very prestigious, influential, distinguished, notable, and prominent. Many thanks to Dr. Jack Mc Manus for his guidance and leadership during my visit with my fellow cohorts. It was, indeed, an amazing experience!

ABOUT THE AUTHOR

Emily Gaddi is a doctoral student at Pepperdine University in their School of Education and Psychology. She is majoring in Organizational Leadership. She earned her Masters degree in 2009 at University of Redlands in Redlands, California. She completed her Bachelors degree with a major in Philosophy at University of Santo Tomas in 1987 Manila, Philippines. Majority of her background is retailing from the buying office and retail management. She is a people person. According to Emily, in order to be successful in your chosen career, you have to be happy and have the ability to make people happy, then excellent productivity will follow.

ACKNOWLEDGEMENTS

When I returned from my May 2012 trip to Washington, I thought about writing about President Obama and his accomplishments based on what Ken Walsh, Chief White House correspondent for the U.S. News & World Report told my fellow cohorts and me. Ken has covered the presidencies from President Reagan to President Obama, and he was very positive about the President. Among other things, he said "The President has a good chance of being re-elected because when he took over the presidency four years ago, our economy was really in bad shape. The auto industry was falling apart. He was able to save Wall Street, and he played an important role in assisting the mortgage crisis that is still going on." This information from Ken inspired me to prepare an outline of a possible book on my way back from Washington D.C. to New York City. I decided to make it simple, easy to read, and easy to understand.

I thank Pepperdine University and all my professors from the University for showing me how to better myself through the many professional development ideas that each one presented in class. They also taught me write scholarly work, and I fell in love with writing!

A special thanks to Brenden Wysocki for being my academic adviser, Christie Dailo, and Maria Brahme for being responsive to all my queries.

I cannot stop writing this acknowledgement section of my book without thanking the many people who had been very supportive of my doctoral studies. Without them, I could never have completed this arduous task: First and foremost, my parents and my two teenagers, Siegfried and Meryl, who are always there for me. My brothers Emil and Emmanuel Gaddi and their respective families. Drs. Abelardo and Zenaida Capati Magat from Atlanta, Georgia, the Capati's of Wisconsin, Uncle Jun and Auntie Connie from Milwaukee, Wisconsin. I also owe a special thanks to

Atty. Carmel Capati, Dr. Anna Capati, and the late Dr. Nazario Capati. The Gaddi family, especially Uncle Israel, for praying for me all the time and his continuous advice about reading the Bible everyday. I would like to recognize Atty. Reginald Pastrana and Atty. Ramon Rana for all the big help that they have done for me. The Prudente family, Dr. Jeffrey Ostriker and family, Msgr. Edgar Pangan, Father Sol Gabriel, Father Joel Reyes, and Barbara Zunich for being there for me whenever I need help.

I have supporters in the Philippines as well. Those who have given me on-going support include John Dayrit, FelmorValles, and Susan Dalida are among my good friends. Chris and Matilde Imbo, the owners of YuuJin Japanese Restaurant in Greenhills, Manila have provided me with love and tender loving care. I also appreciate Tita Cita Rodriguez and Tita Cherry Zapanta for being supportive to my family all the way.

Others who have been there for me are the Reyes family, Atty. Leven Puno and his family, the late Justice Edgar Sundiam, his wife Lourdes Cabrera Sundiam and their two teenagers, Nica and Samantha Sundiam. I have also enjoyed care and concern from Ricardo and Maricel Mariano and their family, Raffy and Lourdes Manoloto and their family, Carlos David and his late wife Aunt Ador, Dr Dennis David, along with Jean and Edwin David and their respective families. I am so thankful for Drs. Renato and Beth Mungcal and all my friends and relatives, my classmates from the University of Santo Tomas, my BA Philosophy class of 1987, St. Marys Academy of Guagua Pampanga, and my fellow cohort from Pepperdine University. All of these people have offered great insight and strength to me. I thank you all.

INTRODUCTION

The purpose of this book is to enlighten my readers about the status of the United States now that President Obama has been in office for nearly four years. As will be shown in the book, there are various categories and events that have affected our economy and the state of the nation during President Obama's first term. There were some excellent things that took place and there were some disastrous events in our lives that have affected his popularity and his chances for re-election. All in all, change has been the key word of this period in history. Finances of the world have changed and so has technology to name but two areas where the changes have been dramatic.

I became interested in writing this book during the past two months as I have been reading and hearing from different forms of media, including the letters published in the New York Times that the President will only be a one time-term president because of the many errors and mistakes he has made. As I read these statements, I found them to be premature, sometimes unjust, often unrealistic, most of the criticisms without proof or knowledge of the circumstances, and in some instances highly discriminatory. After doing research on different issues facing the United States in 2012, it seemed to me that President Obama should be re-elected for his second term because many of the concerns he has been trying to correct started before he took office and could not possibly be resolved during one four-year period. Even had Senator John McCain been elected the problems would have been the same. Senator McCain would have been in the same boat and would have been a disappointment to those who were looking for immediate resolutions to the important problems facing the nation.

I felt the need to speak up and set some of the facts straight. I did not want the American voters to be frustrated, disappointed, and discouraged with four more years of slow progress on the challenges facing the nation if they voted for the Republican candidate. No one, from either party, can change circumstances of the world's economic situation or the recovery from the recent recession quickly. As the President has repeatedly stated, progress is happening, but it will be very slow. As he continually warned his pre-election speeches, revitalizing the United States will not happen overnight; it will take cooperation from many directions and people in order for the country to recover. For this reason, I trust this book will be helpful to getting the current President a second chance to prove himself to the American people. My findings indicate that he has the ability, knowledge, leadership, and plans for on-going progress. I firmly believe that with another four year term, he will prove his worth and be able to demonstrate that he is very proficient and capable of handling our economic crisis.

When the American people decided to vote for President Barack Obama four years ago, they wanted change. They were concerned about the poor economy, energy issues, the environment, the housing market, and foreign policy, health care, the increasing numbers of seniors using social security, and the high unemployment rate. These were concerns that had become serious during the previous administration and were the subjects of the debates and campaigning. Those who voted for President Obama felt he could bring about the changes they were looking to have in their lives and in the welfare of the United States.

In my research, I discovered that the promises of the President were realistic and practical. In his campaigning, his acceptance speech, his after-the-election talks, and the state of the nation addresses, he has continued to focus on the following issues, just as he said he would. His primary areas of concern were and remain:

- The economy
- An extensive re-organization of the Federal budget
- Education
- Energy and environment
- Foreign Policy
- Homeland security
- Labor and union issues
- Science and technology

The economic conditions before the President took office were weak, uncertain, and sluggish. The United States was on the verge of an economic depression. This has not happened! It was partly because of the eight hundred billion dollars financial bailout the country received to anticipate, prevent, and put a stop to further deterioration of the U.S. economy. As stated on President's record of job and the economy, when he took office, the country was losing more than 700,000 jobs per month. He acted quickly to pass the American Recovery and Reinvestment Act, which cut taxes for small businesses and 95 percent of working families. Because such a large percentage of the work force in the United States is employed in companies with 10 or fewer employees, the act affected millions of people as well as some government employees. It included emergency funding to support about 300,000 educators' jobs, more than 4,600 law enforcement positions, and it made investments in the clean energy sector that supported 224,500 jobs through 2010. Through May 2012, the economy has added 4.3 million private sector jobs over 27 consecutive months of job growth. This is a true sign of economic recovery and employment growth.

Who were the people who were looking for change and decided Barack Obama could bring it to them? It was a diverse population. President Obama won 43% of the votes of white voters. Black voters constituted 13 percent of the electorate, which was a 2% rise in the national turnout. Ninety-six percent of these voters supported the President. A stunning 54% of young white voters supported him although he performed slightly worse with older white women. It was such an amazing victory for the President when he became the first African American elected to this highest office in the United States in the 21st century.

From the start of his term, the President has urged everyone to be patient and look for long term solutions. His nomination speech was very encouraging and uplifting because he put an emphasis on the American dream. He continually said he would work hard to help the American people acquire their dream, but that it would not be easy or fast. He explained that he wanted to foster diversified cultural values to keep the American dream dynamic and viable. He even added that our country could once again become the land of opportunities for her citizens and a greener pasture for the people around the globe if we remained patient.

His inauguration speech was very assuring in a sense despite the many challenges that the nation was facing. He was hopeful and optimistic about our country's future under his leadership. He said during this speech:

> "What is required of us now is a new era of responsibility, a recognition, on the part of every American, that we have duties to ourselves, our nation and the world, duties that we do not

grudgingly accept but rather seize grandly, firm in the knowledge that there is nothing so satisfying to the spirit, so defining of our character, than giving our all to a difficult task. This is the price and promise of citizenship".

The main highlights of his inauguration speech were these:

- Economic crisis
- Our nation at war, facing a far-reaching network of violence and hatred
- Mortgage crisis
- Unemployment issues
- Businesses that were failing
- Health care that was too expensive and too exclusive
- Our schools that were failing our students

He also carried these themes forward during his State of the Union Address to the American public. He reminded the listeners that he was determined to set a certain standard about our country's vision that would allow each and everyone to get a fair shake on the economic success regardless of whether the individual was upper, middle, and lower class. The key points of his State of the Union address were the following:

- Calling for extension of mandatory school attendance age.
- Creation of a Trade Enforcement Unit
- Commitment to increasing job training
- Urgent need for immigration overall.

It has been a very tough four years for everyone, but the voters need to remember that President Obama did not cause the problems, he inherited them. We are now making progress toward recovery in many areas of the world, but especially in the United States. I believe that under his leadership, we will continue to do so. I don't think the American people are ready to vote for another change that will start us on a different road toward prosperity. I think they just need to know the facts about how far we've come.

Personally, I was looking for an opportunity to thank the President for helping me and the rest of the American people survive the low American economy and be able to see some positive signs of a bright new future. This book is my way to say, "Thanks for what you are doing, Mr. President."

U.S. ECONOMIC STATUS

Statistically, the United States has shown improvement in some areas of the economy, but there is much more to be accomplished. As this form, distributed by Tampa Bay Times, demonstrates, the growth has been slower than expected. Nevertheless, it does show progress in the right direction for some of the most important factions that affect economic recovery.

Jobs	2008	2009	2010	2011	January 2012	April/May 2012
Unemployment rate	5%	7.8%	9.7%	9.1%	8.3%	8.2%
Broader unemployment rate "U-6"	9.2%	14.2%	16.7%	16.1%	15.1%	14.8%
White unemployment rate	4.4%	7.1%	8.7%	8.1%	7.4%	7.4%
Black unemployment rate	9.1%	12.7%	16.5%	15.7%	13.6%	13.6%
Hispanic unemployment rate	6.5%	10%	12.6%	12%	10.5%	11%
Total private-sector jobs	115.6 M	111 M	106.8 M	108.2 M	110.5 M	111 M
Total government jobs	22.4 M	22.6 M	22.5 M	22.2 M	22 M	22 M
Median weeks unemployed	9	10.7	20.1	21.7	21.1	20.1

Income	2008	2009	2010	2011	January 2012	April/May 2012
Yearly GDP	$13.2 T	$12.7 T	$13.1 T	$13.3 T	—	$13.5 T
Disposable personal income per capita	$33,229	$32,166	$32,481	$32,667	—	$32,677
Personal bankruptcies	1,074,225	1,412,838	1,536,799	1,362,847	—	—
Poverty rate	12.5%	13.2%	14.3%	15.1%	—	—
People receiving food stamps	—	32 M	39 M	44 M	46 M	46 M

Homes	2008	2009	2010	2011	January 2012	April/M 2012
Median home sale price	$232,400	$208,600	$218,200	$240,100	$221,700	$235,700
New homes sold in that month	44,000	24,000	24,000	21,000	23,000	33,000
Existing home sales, annualized	4.2 M	3.8 M	4.2 M	4.5 M	4.6 M	4.6 M
Foreclosure starts	0.88%	1.08%	1.2%	1.27%	0.99%	0.96%

WHERE THE ECONOMY IS TODAY

For ease of discussion and reading, I have briefly covered a large group of the factors—but not all of them—that are affecting the economy today. My purpose is to help the reader understand what role President Obama and Congress had in these changes over the last four years. I decided to list them in alphabetical order rather than try to determine/evaluate which ones where most seriously affecting the economy and American citizens as these rankings changes frequently. By listing important businesses, industries, influential groups, and government entities in alphabetical order, it also makes it easier for the reader to find the ones of interest to that reader and, it is my hope, it will make the book more useful to more individuals.

The brief summary in each of the sections is just that: a brief report on where the sector of the economy is today, four years after President Obama was elected. The short summaries are not meant to cover all of the issues, but just to give the reader one person's analysis of where the US stands today and, in some instances, what the President is trying to do to remedy the situation. Of course, given that much of what he would like to do is actually controlled by Congress, some of the areas the President is trying to improve will take much longer to accomplish.

AIRLINE INDUSTRIES

Whenever there is instability in the economic status of the United States, the airline industry is always one of the first to find itself in a precarious situation. The problem can be caused by higher fuel costs, greater competition, decrease in number of people flying for pleasure, perceived dangers in flying, or a serious terrorist attack or even a well publicized threat. Whatever the cause, the aviation industry often serves as a barometer for the country's future economy. It is an indicator for other businesses as to whether they will do well or not during the next few months. The severity of the airline down turn is sometimes an indicator of very hard economic times to follow.

The changes the airlines make to keep solvent are widely published, such as the surcharges that incurred during these past ten years to keep the airlines afloat, including cancellation of meals and the extra charges for bags. The airlines insist that these are necessary expenses customers must pay to keep the airlines profitable. Thus, the traveler has to be ready for many small extra charges that occur with little notice, but make traveling more expensive. For the most part, these additional expenses have been only applicable to domestic flights.

Due to continual volatility and usually rising fuel costs, most airliners have found it necessary to raise their air fares. I remember travelling to Manila in 2009 when I paid $650.00 for a round trip airfare via Korean Airlines from LAX to Manila. This was the cheapest airfare I have paid since then. This year my round trip ticket to Manila will cost $1,130.00 a raise in price of $480.00. The price was so low in 2009 because the airline was having a promotional to get riders because there was a swine virus epidemic and most of the airline industries were suffering because people were afraid to travel. This is just another example of how world events can affect United States airlines and travel costs. I travel frequently within the Asian region and it has been "business as usual" in the last few years with the different air carriers except they have had to curtail the maximum weight on luggage from 70 lbs. to 50 lbs to help with the rising fuel cost.

Under President Obama's leadership, it was decided to increase taxes on the private jet industry. This seemed reasonable to the average person who does not own a plane, but was very distasteful to plane owners. In the 2013 budget, fees were raised up to $100 per take-off for private jets. The rationale was that these fees could generate up to $7.4 billion over the next ten years and would not impact greatly on the income of those people or companies who were wealthy enough to own private jets.

This type of increase in fees for the richest segment of the population angers many wealthy people. They claim that it is another way to tax them to take care of the population who depends on welfare for income. This is a common complaint of the Republican party about programs the President seeks to implement.

AUTO INDUSTRY

Things in the automobile industry were not looking good across the board before the elections of 2008. When President Obama took office, there were a lot of uncertainties within the United States economy and some of the major builders, such as the auto industry were in grave financial problems. People were afraid to spend their money and were not buying new cars. To lose an industry such as the auto industry would have had serious repercussions across the nation. It would have affected not only those who build vehicles, but also the smaller companies that supply parts for the manufacturing of vehicles, the auto insurance industry, the many car dealerships in the nation, and more. Much of the nation now believes that we should give a "Thank you very much, Mr. President" for saving General Motors and Chrysler Corporation in 2009, which were on the verge of bankruptcy when the President took office in 2009.

As a result of the dire circumstances of the industry, a decision was made to bail them out on a temporary basis. The Federal government granted a $24.9 billion dollars for the auto industries, with $17.4 billion for General Motors and Chrysler, $6 billion for GMAC, and $1.5 billion for Chrysler Financial. This has turned out to be a wise financial move. It saved the automobile industry, their employees, and the communities in which the vehicles are built. The principle decision behind this bailout for the auto industry was to support and accommodate operating cash for both companies and to make auto loans easier for customers who are qualified. This plan worked and some of the companies have already returned the money that was loaned to them.

If not have been with the financial bailout for the auto industry, I don't know where the nation would stand at this time. Those who said, "Let them fail," were probably not considering the consequences that would have followed like a "house made of cards." Regardless of which party had won the Presidential race in 2008, things would have been the same. It would be unrealistic to blame President Obama for this economic mess. The country was already in disarray when he was running for office and the former administration did nothing to resolve the issues.

The readers should also keep in mind that the nation was at war on several fronts—all far away from the mainland—at this time. When the country is at war, it has a tendency to deeply affect the economy. It is very expensive to be at war when the country is sending our troops to the target places, and the cost of the armaments and different necessary equipment is costing millions each year. We cannot send our troops into war without proper backing. This affects the whole economy, but these wars, too, were in place when the new President took office. He was not responsible for their start, but his administration was responsible for the care and safety of troops. The President and his advisors are making good progress toward ending the United States involvement in overseas conflicts, but this, too, will take time as we have made promises to the countries where we are fighting.

As stated earlier, this administration has made a good start, but will need the second term to complete the job. Making another change in leadership will only slow down the progress that has been made so far.

BABY BOOMERS

Young males returning to the United States, Canada, and Australia following tours of duty overseas during World War II began their families, which brought about a significant number of new children. This dramatic increase in the number of births from 1946 to 1964 (1947 to 1966 in Canada and 1946-1961 in Australia) is called the Baby Boom era (Rosenberg, 2009). Those born during this era have become known as the Baby Boomers and they are now reaching middle age. Their working days are numbered and they will soon be eligible for social security and collecting their pensions. These baby boomers are about my age. To us, the best Presidents in our lifetime have been Presidents Reagan and Clinton because there was consistent economic growth, they were able to curb inflation somewhat, the unemployment rate was relatively low, wages were high, and the country had a very strong national defense.

What is happening now to the economy is not unique in the United States. Such economic recessions have occurred many times in our country's history and because history repeats itself no one should be surprised. But we Baby Boomers are. We have lived in such prosperity that we thought it would go on forever. We were fortunate to live during the most financially successful period in the history of the United States. Our parents had much more than their parents and they wanted even more prosperity for us. They continued to give and we continued to take and to buy. We were not aware what an economic recession could do to our jobs, home prices, opportunities for career advancement, and even cause the inability to buy whatever we wanted.

We had not learned for example, when World War I and World War II started that the United States was just recovering from an economic downturn. We did not realize that the country only made a strong economic recovery after the wars ended. We did not understand that wars often follow a massive worldwide economic depression. We did not consider that war will always be very expensive and the nation always has to pay a very high premium, including a dramatic increase in overall national debt. We Baby Boomers had never suffered from lack so we did not realize that as Americans we will be impacted by whatever consequences that came along, including what happened in other parts of the world. This includes drought, poor government leadership, economic problems, wars and civic unrest in other countries.

It happened before in the United States and to the older generation it is not surprising that it is happening now, but as a Baby Boomer we had not experienced this type of almost-depression so we were shocked. We were certainly not prepared to cope with it successfully. We did not have the financial savings mind-set of our ancestors so we were dependent on week-to-week large incomes. We thought that there would always be jobs and money to buy "toys" of every type. Thus, any President who was challenged by the United States and world economy since 2009 would have found it difficult to please many segments of the nation, but especially the Baby Boomers who were growing older and expecting to live at the same high level.

Whoever was in charge of the country would have found it difficult to make changes rapidly or to please this segment of the population. The end results would have been the same. There would be a very slow growth in the recovery of the nation's economic situation and this would have dire consequences on education, health services, unemployment rates, the construction and housing market. This has been further complicated by what is going on in Europe and Asian financial markets.

Under President Obama's leadership, recovery seems to be happening. Everyday we see that the policies put in place by the President and his cabinet members are beginning to work, but for many Baby Boomers the improvement in the economy will come too late. They have already lost their homes, had the cars repossess, lost their well paying jobs and become disillusioned with the government. Like their grandparents, they will have to learn to do with much less. It remains to be seen if they can do it or if they will continue to look for a quick-fix for their problems by voting for a change in the government, particularly the President.

CONSTRUCTION INDUSTRY

When times are good and things are going well, the construction industry is at its peak, jobs are plentiful, construction workers are making excellent wages, and the industries that support construction, such as lumber and construction materials are doing well financially. But when there is a downturn in the economy, one of the first industries to suffer is construction. It is not a good, sustaining career because there is no stability; it is dependent on the nation's ups and downs economically. Because of the economic recession we are experiencing and the mortgage crisis that is going on, it should have been obvious that the construction industry would be sluggish and nearly comatose, and that this condition would last until the economy could once again support new buildings and houses. Unfortunately, many of the people heavily involved in construction are of the Baby Boomer generation and they have not paid much attention to the past history of construction and were not aware that it could happen to them as well.

The people working in this kind of industry are now being forced to "think outside the box" about how to survive and to think further about how to better prepare themselves for the future because the construction industry is always vulnerable to downturns. The people connected to this industry are learning from this experience that it is necessary in this day and age to aim higher and be prepared for changes. Personally, I come from a well educated background wherein most of the family members are doctors, lawyers, and business people, but I ended up working for different retailers. These retailers, like the construction industry, have no permanence. Given that there is no steadiness in the retail industry even if you own the company and many large retailers, such as Circuit City and even Sears have failed or endured significant setbacks, I had to find a way to take myself to the next level and not depend on the retail business to provide for my future. I decided to protect myself and my family by investing in my professional development.

I currently own a few properties in Palos Verdes. I was able to acquire them because I had the minimum down payment and an excellent credit, but the downturn in the economy has made it difficult to acquire additional ownership. I should have known that this high-flying economy was too good to last. If I had studied more economics, I would have known that there are many ups and downs financially in the history of the United States. I should have thought about something like happening to the economy, but I, like many Baby Boomers assumed that it would just go on the same way, with me getting more and more prosperous. Well, the downturn in the economy did happen, and I learned that I really need to be educated.

So, I decided to enroll at the University of Redlands in their School of Business and from there, I fell in love with graduate school. I have almost completed my doctoral studies at Pepperdine University and I feel much more secure now about my future. Having a doctoral degree is the highest educational attainment that a person can achieve and it will allow me to find many more lucrative professions in the future. Based on my experiences without a degree, I would urge the people from the construction industry to seek professional advice from friends and family to help them get over this downturn in the economy. As I am finding out, life gets more difficult as years goes by and having an education is a must in today's economy. Getting an education is not impossible for anyone in the United States. There is always financial aid available to every American no matter what their circumstances are. Everyone should take advantage of it. We are very lucky that we live in this great country where there is such an aid available from our government.

I originally came from a developing country where it is so different. If a parent wants to send their children to school, they must be able to pay for all of it personally. They do not have the kind of luxury that the United States government is offering to all. Life can be so much better and easier if we decide to invest in our future. In the meantime, those in the construction business and those who depend on it, such as retailers who sell carpet and window coverings or roofing, need to always be on guard against the next downturn in business.

EDUCATIONAL CRISIS

Learning is the number one priority in many families; it is the backbone of the nation. Every President seeks to be called the education President and to give full support to helping educational institutions. But what happens when the finances of the country are at a low ebb and the federal government is not able to give as much money to the states for education? Well, the individual states must find their own ways to fund education, but when the economy is slow and the tax base is down this is difficult to do. Everyone suffers!

It leads to teachers being laid off because of massive budget cuts, which is really disappointing to everybody because teachers are not supposed to be laid off. It was thought that teachers always had job security. And what about all of the new teachers-in-training who are coming out of college? Where will they find teaching jobs? This type of event shocks all levels of the population. It interferes with the President's wish to retain teachers and have senior teachers act as mentors to the newly graduated educators. It leads to state universities raising the cost of tuition and mandates that they enroll fewer students. It leads to support personnel being laid off and causes those who are left assume too many responsibilities. In some cities, it leads to public schools asking parents to pay for the student supplies. In other words, the situation becomes tenuous for administrators, teachers, students, and parents.

Conforming to a 2010 world education ranking from the OECD (Organization for Economic Co-operation and Development), the United States now ranks 14th out of the 34 countries included on the list. As a nation that has prided itself on being one of the world's elitist countries in education, it is discouraging to fall to just average. This spurs a number of questions. The first questions that's on everyone's mind is, "How did this happen"? It is now known that since the Bush Administration implemented the *No Child Left Behind* law, our educational system has seen a severe dip in ranking and graduation statistics. The number of drop-outs continues to increase in inner city schools, especially among black and Latino males. According to a report in the Los Angeles Times in July 2012, on an average school day, 7,000 students across the nation drop out of school. And, conforming to the Huffington Post, "four out of five schools may be tagged as failures this year under provisions of the Bush—era *No Child Left Behind* law". The Huffington Post, further reports that the percentage of schools that are failing has jumped from thirty-seven percent to a staggering eighty-two percent nationwide. This is not the President's doing.

President Obama is aware of how important education is to the nation and is pushing for a better way to prepare high school graduates for college and careers. He is urging congress to create a new educational plan so that our nation's students and school systems don't fall behind in the 21st century. This is consistent with President Obama's 2012 State of the Union Address, in which he stated, "At this defining moment in our history, America faces few more urgent challenges than preparing our children to compete in the global economy. The decisions our leaders make about education in the coming years will shape our future for generations to come. It will help determine not only whether our children have the chance to fulfill their God-given potential or whether our workers have a chance to build a better life for their families, but whether we as a nation will remain in the 21st century the kind of global economic leader that we were in the 20th century. The rising importance of education reflects the new demands of our new world".

Like many of the nation's educators, President Obama realizes that education is the key to everything. It is a key away from poverty, a key to a better career, and a key to a better life. He and his advisors are on the right track and need the full support of Congress to make the necessary changes to education happen. If we help him to succeed, the educational hardships will be temporary, but if we change leadership now, it will take a new President time to prepare new legislation to improve education. Our students don't have this time to waste. This is just one more reason why we need to continue with our current Presidential team.

EMPLOYMENT

Many in the media are writing that the unemployment rate in the fall of 2013 will become the predictor of whether President Obama will be re-elected in November 2012. The current national rate of unemployment across the country is 8.1% and is expected to be lower from now until election time, but not much. In the second quarter, weak consumer spending held growth to an annual rate of just 1.5 percent, even less than the two percent of the first quarter. This means that high unemployment isn't going to end quickly. The rate of unemployment will probably remain about the same as long as the economy grows as slowing as it is doing according to Dan Greenhaus, Chief Economic Strategist for BTIG LLC.

This is an extremely challenging issue on the part of the President. Washington is interested in putting the America worker back to work, but it is unlikely that the federal government, the White House or Congress can or will do anything soon because of the historically high budget deficits. It is difficult to spend more money when we are already so deeply in debt. While the economy has not worsened while President Obama has been in office, many voters were looking for quick answers and solutions to the unemployment rate. These unrealistic voters do not realize how slow the government works, how much it takes to make changes to the economy, or how little power the President has to make change without support of Congress. They are not aware of how much effort it takes to even make a slow growth in the economy possible. Most economists find it difficult to explain this information in general terms, but that is needed to make people understand that a 2.4 percent growth in 2010 was actually a "huge" number. Then the growth fell to 1.8 percent in 2011, roughly the same as it grew in the first months of 2012. This was not good news for the President or the country.

I was privileged to hear Ken Walsh, Chief White House correspondent for U.S. News & World Report, when he spoke to my fellow cohorts and me when we were in Washington DC in May, 2012. Mr. Walsh has covered the presidencies from President Reagan to President Obama, and he told us, "The President has a better chance of being re-elected because when he took over the presidency four years ago, our economy was really in bad shape. The auto industry was falling apart and he saved it. He was able to save Wall Street, and he played an important role in assisting the mortgage crisis that is still going on." I was happy he was so positive that the President will be re-elected, but I realized that he, too, had reservations. My only reservation is this: "If the stock market plummets towards the third quarter of 2012 or if the stock market becomes bear for the rest of the year, President Obama will lose the election." This cycle that has happened to many of the incumbent Presidents of this country and is not considered a good sign of prosperity. Fortunately, the stock market has taken several rallies in July, 2012 and appears to be stronger than it was at the beginning of the year. If this trend continues, this will be good news for the President.

The additional factors of concern regarding employment growing are the severe drought in the middle of the country which will push food prices higher, the sluggish recovery rates for manufacturing, home and auto sales, and the fact that pay is not keeping up with the rate of inflation. While there is so much uncertainty in many industries and businesses, employers are reluctant to hire new employees. Many economists are saying that the Feds may launch another round of bond buying in September. The aim is to drive long-term interest rates even lower and encourage more borrowing and spending on the part of the consumer. If this happens, it should help the unemployment rate decrease as the interest rate, the stock market and unemployment rate are closely joined. These would all be positive help in the re-election of President Obama.

ENTREPRENEURSHIP

President Obama continues to say how much he believes in our nation's creativity and the power of the people to use their ingenuity to find ways to use their entrepreneurial skills to overcome the unemployment rates. At every opportunity and rally he encourages those without employment to "think outside the box." He points out that Americans are truly a genius when it comes to ingenuity. For the entire history of the country, Americans have been brilliant and resourceful in pursuit of making a living for their family. It has led the United States to become a super power among nations in just over two hundred years, and has led the United States to become among the richest countries. Many countries want to emulate this ability to be flexible and creative, but most of them cannot replicate this country's entrepreneurial success because the government and the mindset of the laws of the United States are unique and uncommon. It is only in America that people from all over the world can make things happen. We are such a remarkable country because her entrepreneurs are visionaries. President Obama has often said that we need to have laws and policies that are supportive and accommodating to entrepreneurs because they are the main engine in the success of our country's economic recovery. This means that the laws and taxes have to be favorable to the entrepreneur.

America is all about innovation. We are committed to ensuring that our economy will be the strongest economy in the entire world. We need the President to be successful in his campaign for "Start-up America," one of the strongest initiatives President Obama has introduced during his term in the White House. He and his advisors understand that it is through the ambition and ingenuity of the thousands of small entrepreneurs that the country can develop new ideas and new types of startup businesses throughout the country. These small companies, that often begin in garages or at the kitchen table, have frequently lead to strong, large businesses that do millions of dollars annually. Great examples are Facebook, Apple, and Thirty-One, businesses that were not even thought of before an enterprising entrepreneur put his/her dreams to reality.

Americans may not be able to get a job doing what they have always done, but they have the will and the power to create job through entrepreneurship, education, and mentorship. The President wants to encourage investments for research and development, which can generate innovate start-ups and create new industries. Lastly, the President wants to boost collaboration between large companies and startups. His ideas have great potential and he needs time to implement some of them. A second term would provide this opportunity.

FINANCIAL AND BANKING INDUSTRY CRISIS

President Obama's issuance of the Emergency Economic Stabilization Act of 2008, which was better known as the stimulus plan, was a response to a collapsing economy. If this had been allowed to continue it would have brought economic upheaval around the world. As a result of this stimulus package, the United States Treasury gave money to mortgage companies and inserted money into some of the banks so they would not collapse as 600 other banks did in two years, 2008-2010. The stimulus plan was designed to rescue the American people and the country's economy. The main purposes of the financial bailout were these: purchasing bad assets, reducing uncertainty regarding the worth of the remaining assets, and restoring confidence in the credit market. The goal of financial bailout was to release the banks from their financial burdens as more and more homeowners and businesses went into foreclosure. For some people, the bailout worked, but for others it did not because some of the banks refused to approve any loans for too long a period of time. Nevertheless, if the government had not implemented the $800 billion bailout plan, the results would have been a financial crisis and things would be a lot worse now. It was necessary for the government to step in to avoid an economic depression. Despite what the critics say about the stimulus plan, it was essential during the financial crisis to maintain stability, keep credit markets open, ensure normal operations in the financial markets and ensure financial liquidity worldwide.

Without the implementation of the stimulus package, the United States might have been caught in a depression as severe as the one of

1918 when all the banks failed. Those who supported letting the "chips fall where they may" felt that failure of large companies and banks as well as financial institutions would not have been as serious as President Obama thought it might be. Personally, I am happy that he and congress made the decision to protect our large companies and banks. To have ignored this serious plight to the welfare of the country would have been irresponsible.

FOREIGN MONEY CRISIS

The foreign money crisis was beginning long before President Obama took office. As we have all observed it has brought serious financial instability all over the globe. Regardless of who won the Presidential election in 2008, nothing the United States did or not do was going to fix the problems of Europe and Asia. The foreign financial instability needed to be addressed and resolved by those countries who were involved in causing the situation. The financial condition of the United States, as well as many of the developing countries were in a very bad shape. The United States was in no position to help all of them. Some countries were able to recover and others, such as Greece and France are still struggling to remedy their finances. At the same time, the United States was enduring an ailing economy primarily because we were at war, but also because there was several major financial scandals going on caused by greedy people and financial institutions. The USA was overspending on the war, aid to dependent countries, and other major obligations.

To blame President Obama for these conditions shows a lack of understanding of the situation. He has been accused of surrounding himself with native academicians, lawyers, politicians, bureaucrats, and left-leaning contributors. To this accusation, one must ask, "If you were in charge of the financial matters of the United States, with whom wouldyou consult?"

None of the major financial experts or economists can agree on the proper solution to help the nations of the world get out of this mess so it seems to me that he has chosen a wide-range of highly educated people to assist him understand the situation and make proper decisions.

HEALTH INITIATIVE

On March 23, 2010, The Affordable Healthcare Act became the law of the land. In keeping with the news on article on CBS, "Health Care Reform Bill Summary: A Look At What's in the Bill," the initial cost of the new law is estimated to cost around nine-hundred-forty-billion dollars. Over the course of ten years it would decrease the nation's national debt by one-hundred-thirty billion dollars. After another decade it is estimated to lower the deficit by another 1.2 trillion dollars. In addition, the new health law also provides coverage for thirty-two million American without health care insurance.

Initially many people were disillusioned by the new health care law because they were led to believe that their medical coverage would change if this legislation were passed. The notion that anything might change made them skeptical and nervous. It was especially hard for seniors to understand how the legislation would affect them. A letter from the Resurgent Republic attempted to reassure some of this law's most advocate protestors through education about the law. An article addressed the issue: " . . . what changes are on the horizon due to Obama Care." Still many segments of the population, especially the medical professionals several expressed concern. Some people thought that their health care coverage would not stay the same, including changes to doctor access or quality of care. The medical professionals expressed concerns that they would lose a great deal of money because the government would be determining what they could charge. The article reminded seniors that the proposed reforms would not affect those currently on Medicare or those expected to enroll in the next decade. It explained that should they choose to do so, they can remain in the present system" (Lohuizen, 2012). All in all, President Obama's health care reform seems to be doing the right thing. In theory, it can help balance our national deficit. For those with existing medical coverage, they can keep their current health plans. The thirty-two million Americans who cannot afford health insurance now will be covered by this new health law. With health care reform making a positive change in the lives of millions American lives, there is yet another reason why President Obama should stay in office for another term.

HEALTH INDUSTRY

It was definitely a victory for the President to have his Health Care Reform Law initiative upheld and confirmed by the Supreme Court. This was an excellent accomplishment for the President, and showed the leadership of Vice President Joe Biden, Secretary of Health and Human Services, Kathleen Sebelius, and the rest of the President's cabinet members. This means that the health care program, known as Obamacare, now can move forward and has a chance to be successful. It will have implementation problems as all such huge government undertakings do, but it gives home to those with no health care insurance.

I just can imagine the how a huge population of Americans, especially women who cannot afford health insurance, feel now that they will have easy access to preventive care at no cost, such as check-ups, mammograms, colonoscopies, pre-existing conditions, HIV screening, immunization, autism screening for children, and all the preventive care services that were not affordable before. Now each and everyone will be given the opportunity to afford them. Millions of Americans who have not been able to afford health insurance in the past will benefit from the Supreme Court ruling. Because both of my parents are now senior citizens, this means that they will be able to secure prescription drug benefits. All in all, it will mean millions of dollars in health care savings to the rest of the senior elders. The President really cares about the little people who don't have the means to live healthy lives without assistance from government programs. It is through the Obama care that millions of Americans will be able to enjoy the many benefits of living healthy. We never had this kind of luxury before, but because of our President, we can now take advantage of the Obama care because it was design to help millions of Americans.

THE HOMELESS AND THE WORKING POOR

As stated in the National Alliance to End Homelessness, on any given night there are approximately 636,017 homeless people either searching for shelter or wandering around the streets of the United States looking for a safe place to sleep. The numbers range from children to military veterans, from whole families to homeless individuals. Statistics from the SOH 2012: Chapter One—Homelessness Counts revealed: "A majority of the homeless population is composed of individuals (63 percent or 399,836 people). The number of people in families with children makes up 37 percent of the overall population, a total of 236,181 people in 77,186 family households. Of these homeless individuals, about one quarter of the population are chronically homeless (107,148 people)" ("SOH").

In 2010, the Obama administration revealed a plan to end child and family homeless within ten years; in conjunction the plan would end chronic and veteran homelessness in five years. In 2012, it seems the Obama Administration's plan is well under way. An article from the Huffington Post reveals that, "On any given night in January, 67,495 homeless veterans were sleeping on the streets, a 56 percent decline since the president took office, according to the Annual Homelessness Assessment Report to Congress" ("President"). With the sudden progress of the Obama Administration's homeless plan it seems that the majority of homelessness could really be gone in approximately ten years.

In an article from *News Max*, "Ranks of Working Poor Growing Under Obama," it, revealed that currently the working poor rate is seven percent of the population. In 2010, the annual mean income for a single person was $10,830 and an income for a family of four was $22,050. Unfortunately the Obama Administration has proposed a plan that will cut funding to the working poor. According to the Huffington Post article, "Obama Budget Proposal: Cuts To Target Working Poor, Middle Class and Students" the proposed spending plan to Congress will cut funding to programs that assist the working poor, help the needy heat their homes, and expand access to graduate-level education". This is a risky political move in an election year and can have a detrimental side effect to President Obama's election. On the other hand, it is in line with one of the two top priorities of the American voter: to reduce the national deficit. Cutting out these programs will ultimately reduce the national deficit by 1.1 trillion. It is not possible to continue the programs and reduce the deficit by 1.1 trillion in such a short time. The question then to consider is this: "Is it worth the saving if the working poor and their families must suffer for it"?

HOUSING INDUSTRY

The housing industry is probably one of the biggest challenges that President Obama's administration has had to face since he took office in 2009. Its collapse was one of the biggest catastrophes in the United States in recent time and affected every state and almost all other industries that are connected to it in any way. The bursting of the bubble of housing prices was devastating to so many families, their income, and their financial situation. To say it succinctly, "It went to hell!"

Rectifying the problem of the housing market has not been easy for the President. In fact, it is still not recovered and many economists say that until the housing market recovers we are not out of the recession, nor can we expect to get out of the recession. There are so many key players who were involved in the mess: the banks who made loans to people they could not afford and with too high payments, the construction industry that had to quit building as no one could buy, the realtors across the country whose huge incomes suddenly dropped, the mortgage companies who financed new and re-sold home and then collapsed, and those who became unemployed when their companies failed or downsized.

Of course, the President was aware of the situation and he and his advisors tried to implement several plans to help millions of homeowners save their homes. In some respects he did a fair job with the plans that were implemented, but in some respects the plans failed as the banks did not release the monies to those who were entitled to it and refused to modify loans or make new loans for millions. In some areas there are so many homes empty waiting for the bank to take over that the bank officials have lost track of some.

My neighbor's sister stopped making mortgage payments on her home in January of 2009. She is still living in the house and has yet to hear from the bank that they are foreclosing on the property. She is saving money to buy a new house when the bank tells her to move out. She is just another example of the problems the banks are having with the loans they gave. Some other people were fortunate; for them mortgage and principal reductions took place as the programs mandated. For millions of others, however, no relief was available even though they qualified according to the plan. No one seems to know why the banks refused to handle the program as planned, but the results were serious and many people lost their homes while money to rescue them was available, but not being used for its intended purpose.

Some homeowners whose homes were foreclosed were, in part, responsible for what happened to them. They were not being realistic about their financial situation when they bought their dream house. The banks were equally responsible because they made loans without doing due diligence on the buyers ability to re-pay their loan. In many other instances, a loss of a job and the inability to find a new one caused the family to lose their home.

It was very sad, of course, but each buyer must take into consideration how much they could afford to pay and assume personal responsibility if they over-bought. Over-buying hurt millions in the end and cost banks a fortune. The foreclosure rate, which appears to be declining, is a good measure of how much the economy has recovered. In some states there are positive signs that the programs implemented by President Obama are starting to be successful. In other states, including California, there are still many foreclosures taking place and others that are expected to take place in the next two years.

Blaming President Obama for the failure of banks to use the available funds to bail people out of their financial problems does not make sense. His programs should have worked if the banks had cooperated and done their job.

IMMIGRATION

In my opinion, one of the best immigration reforms that ever happened in the history of this country was the decision to end the deportation of younger illegal immigrants who came to the United States as children. For many of these youth, the United States is the only home they have ever known and they have little, in any, affiliation with their native country. For those youth who have not been in trouble and want to continue higher education, this is a "dream come true." It may allow them to apply for financial aid and other benefits that they have been denied because they were not born in the United States. The President is always very sympathetic to those who are less fortunate because he was raised by a single parent and fully understands how it is to be a family that is struggling.

As an immigrant, I have been quite pleased that the President has always been candid and equitable about his position on immigration. He has been efficient, capable, and unprejudiced to all younger immigrants and has worked for them because he wants equal opportunity for all people who live in this country and support its laws. It is entirely possible that some of these younger illegal immigrants will be able to find the solution to some of the country's problems in the future. Granting work permits to the younger illegal immigrants who are doing well in school is one of the most important benefit that any illegal immigrant can obtain. It provides a way to succeed and be a contributing member of society. These young beneficiaries would have greater access to educational opportunities and jobs. As they mature, the United States will be able to benefit from these people through their taxable income. And the young adults may obtain the opportunity to become citizens of the United States and vote.

From an early age, I have watched how the different political parties treat immigrants. I have observed that not only President Obama has a heart for people in need, but it seems this is the philosophy of the entire Democratic Party. I have been most impressed by the way they think. To me they are liberal, humanitarian, and broad minded toward the needs of all the people.

It is this Dream Act, which the President introduced, that will allow legalized immigrants to invest in the United States economy. Not all immigrants are poor, many come from a very affluent background. They can now use that money to further their education. The act will not only keep talented students in the US to help the country become more prosperous, it will assist the United States maintain its super power status in the world. The Dream Act will aid the military recruiting teams as well because many of these younger immigrants from different countries will show their appreciation by enlisting and serving their new country. In return, the United States, that was once known as the "melting pot of the world" be able to learn more about different cultures. This will make it easier to negotiate with different cultures when Americans are doing foreign travel and business.

I applaud President Obama for making this Dream Act available to the youth who are seeking to be an asset to America.

MID-LIFE AMERICANS

"I don't care whether or not you are driving a hybrid or an SUV, if you're headed for a cliff, you have to change direction to survive. That's what the American people called for in November 2008 and that's what we intend to deliver" In 2008, Barack Hussein Obama was elected as the 44th President of the United States for a new generation of Americans. According to the news article "Young Voters in the 2008 Election," 66% of those under age 30 voted for President Obama making the disparity between young voters and other age groups larger than in any presidential election . . . ("Young"). The disaster Obama inherited was that the Bush administration left the American economy in disarray.

In an article by Joseph Sitglitz, "The Economic Consequences of Mr. Bush," he identifies the repercussions of the failing Republican party: "a tax code that has become hideously biased in favor of the rich; a national debt that will probably have grown 70 percent by the time this president leaves Washington; a swelling cascade ofmortgage defaults; a record near-$850 billion trade deficit; oil prices that are higher than they haveever been; and a dollar so weak that for an American to buy a cup of coffee in London or Paris—oreven the Yukon—becomes a venture in high finance" (Stiglitz). Due to the incompetence of the Bush administration, Obama was able to capitalize on the disillusioned American youth by promising them change, renewal in the government, and hope for a better America. America, a nation of immigrants, for nearly two-hundred years has had the face of a white man. This American generation has proved that we have all moved past the race issue, and our greatest evidence is our current commander-in-chief.

With the 2012 presidential elections inching its way as the days pass, President Obama's popularity with the youth and young adult is coming into question due to our 50% increase in national debt, lack of jobs, and a handful of other problems that may disenchant some of his former supporters. Boaz's article, "President Obama and the Youth Vote," argues otherwise: "PresidentObama still gets 64 percent of the youth vote . . . the President has been working hard to fire up his youth base. He's stumped the country promising to keep interest rates low on student loans, and every voter likes free money. And then perhaps more importantly, he re-established his cool by endorsing gay marriage. Hope and change are back. For many young voters, this reconnected them to the hip young President Obama of 2008" (Boaz, 2012).

Thanks to the re-vamping of his 2012 campaign and the many blunders being made by those who would oppose him, it seems that more likely than not, President Obama will stay for a second term. The fact of the matter is, the President Obama will continue to play his strengths in the coming months of the presidential campaign. Due to President Obama's charisma he is able to rally, inspire, and make people believe that he is the best choice for our country. America is a country of aesthetics and for generations, America has been led by men of Caucasian backgrounds. What better way to show we are still a country of change? By reelecting the man who made us all believe that there is still hope and that everything isn't simply black and white.

PRINT MEDIA / PUBLISHING BUSINESSES

Thanks to technology, the global media landscape, like everything else, is forever evolving. In a digitized world, what is the status of print media? How are the changes affecting the economy of the United States? The printed word is one area that has been essential in the revolution of the world during the last five hundred years, it is the printed word. Printing technology simply made it easy for the world to share knowledge and further the cause of human civilization.

This need for the written word changed towards the end of the nineteenth century when radio became a household item. At first it looked like news in print would soon be history, but contrary to all expectations and predictions, the print news media thrived. Then television arrived, but print media continued strongly. The invention of the Internet made some inroads on print media, but did not take a huge toll. With the invention and acceptance of cell phones, i-pads, and portable computers, everything is changing dramatically. Newspapers and magazines are in a steady decline, and the economic recession has only added to their bag of woes.

One major reason for this decline is the ever-changing tastes and reading habits of the people in the developed world. They are reading less and increasingly consuming their news other ways. Because of the recession, advertising revenues have dropped significantly and this has impacted on printing companies. The latest figures of the Publisher Information Bureau of the United States indicate that till September 2009, magazines in the United States have seen a whopping 27 percent drop in the number of advertisement pages translating into a 20 percent drop in revenue.

In consonance with Huffington Post, new resources are using innovative models such as using unpaid bloggers; this totals about half of their writing team today. With this unique system they are one of the few print media outlets making a profit. President Obama wrote for them before the election and it has become the most visited blog on the Internet!Professionally managed blogs and aggregators that offer relevant video and audio inputs (live or recorded) are taking over the place of print media and people using the Kindle or the Nook are getting their daily news information this way.

Learning about the upcoming election and what the candidates are doing and saying can be almost instantaneous. There is no need to wait for the morning paper to tell you about it. To counter this, five of the big magazine publishers in the US—Condé Nast, Meredith Corp., News Corp., Time Inc. and Hearst Corp have teamed up together to form a 'digital storehouse' to provide digital content to consumers across media like phones, e-book and so forth so that they won't lose contact with their former readers. It's a new way of getting news faster, with on-site videos of the situation. As a result, print media is suffering and looking for new ways to compete. And the new news media outlets have made it necessary for the President and Congress to enact new laws to protect the citizens.

REAL ESTATE INDUSTRY

The rising pricesof the housing market was out of control in 2009. The interest rates were reasonably low, and home buyers and investors were buying houses with small down payments and then trying to sell these purchases in a year or two for a good profit. In many cases, the buyers were using equity in their primary homes to make these purchases and were depending on the rent and their lucrative jobs to make the payments on the new houses until they could re-sell them. It worked well for several years and then suddenly everything changed. Just like it always does in the real estate market. In the meantime, realtors and other investors began to leverage the homes they had just purchased to purchase even more inventory. When the bubble burst in the real estate market—as these bubbles do every few years—thousands of people lost all of their investments and their primary homes. It was and is a nationwide disaster. The President did not cause the bubble to burst; it was greed and the inability of the market to sustain those high prices. When the fall to the real estate market happened, thousand of realtors were without any income. They could not finance their "castle of homes." The results to the Real Estate Industry was disastrous and it still has not recovered although just recently I saw an advertisement by a large real estate company for salesman.

In the eastern section of the United States there are indicators that the worst of the housing slump is ending, but in the western part of the United States sales of used and new homes remains flat. As a result of this, a lot of mortgage brokers and underwriter who were "raking in the money" lost everything as well because they were not using good financial business rules. They were loaning money to anyone who wanted to buy a house.

President Obama and Congress tried to fix the housing problems though new legislations, but it was not as successful as they had hoped.

Then the President enacted other policies to rescue the millions of Americans who could not afford to pay their mortgages. While the plans sounded attractive and alluring, the success rate has been quite slow. In fact, the fall of the housing market in the 2000's is one of the biggest real estate disasters to ever hit the United States. This is particularly true in areas where manufacturing plants have closed or the biggest industry in the area (i.e. a lumber mill) closed.

To re-start the real estate market President Obama plan was to help millions of responsible Americans refinance their mortgages by lowering their interest rate and providing a principal reduction to those homeowners who are underwater. If this had worked as planned, millions of homeowners would have been able to prevent foreclosure. It should have stabilized the housing market and helped to improve the economic situation in the country. There is now a third plan being introduced to try to help the homeowners who are in financial difficulty, but it remains to be seen whether the banks and lending institutions will adopt the plan and make it work. The President tried to find a way to help homeowners escape foreclosure because it is so detrimental to all aspects of the economy when homeowners lose their dream home. In most instances, they have worked and saved for it and all of a sudden, because of unavoidable circumstances, the American dream is shuttered.

Economists agree that the President did the right thing. They are not in agreement as to why the banks and financial institutions have not done their part. Saving the real estate market and preventing foreclosures would be an excellent way to help Americans restore their confidence in the American economy. It would be another way to help those who have suffered through loss of income and financial stability be proud of their country even in this tough and trying economic times.

The President's effort to make the real estate market viable again makes me proud to be an American. The policy of good will toward all residents has always been the cornerstone of this President's term.

RESTAURANT INDUSTRY

Despite the acceptance of the President's new health care law by the Supreme Court by the smallest of margins (one vote), enacting the law will face a lot of political backlash from service industries, including the restaurant industry. A newspaper article, "Restaurants opposed to health care law ruling," states that although they are looking to help provide better health coverage for their employees, the new law makes it more difficult for them to financially recover." Another article from *Grub Street New York* said, "It didn't take long for the restaurant industry to express deep disappointment after the Supreme Court announced its decision today to uphold President Obama's future health-care plans." That's because, according to the law, food and drink establishments with 50 or more full-time employees must now offer health insurance to all of their workers. This includes all of those restaurants that hire many part time or seasonal employees as well as their full-time employees. In addition to the restaurant industry, many other factions of the food industry are less than happy with the food safety fees requested by the President's administration during the past several years. They claim that the new fees, combined with the need to provide health care for all workers, will make it impossible for them to make ample profits.

In an article from Food Safety News, "Food Industry Tells Administration, No Food Safety Fees" the request comes from numerous industries, including American Frozen Food Institute, the American Meat Institute, the Juice Products Association, the United Fresh Produce Association and the Pet Food Institute. The petition they sent to the President said, in part "We respectfully ask that you make securing adequate congressional funding for U.S. Food and Drug Administration (FDA) food safety activities one of your highest priorities rather than proposing any new food taxes or regulatory fees on consumers and food makers . . ." With all this political backlash coming towards President Obama from the food and restaurant industry, it has tainted his popularity with this segment of American voters.

RETAIL INDUSTRY

Regardless of who is the President of the country, retailing is retailing. When I say this, I mean, there is no stability in this industry. It is the worst career you can have if you are looking for a career that brings stability and a peaceful life. In this industry, where I spent the majority of my working time, there is often conflict among the staff and management and between the management team members. People in this industry will "kill" each other to ensure that they have a job and that their pathway to upper management is not stopped. Personally, I respect everyone in the retail sector and I love all of them and want them to secure happiness and good wages. Happiness to many retailers is positive cash flow, excellent productivity, and the ability to make everyone happy whether they are customers, vendors, and/or their respective employees.

Most, but certainly not all, of the big box retailers have survived this great economic recession, but for them to remain afloat, they need to urge President Obama to do the following to promote and create jobs in the industry.

- Sales tax fairness. Legislation is needed so on-line retailers start charging taxes. This is needed so the main street retailers can stay in the game with them.
- Corporate tax reform. There is a need to eliminate deductions and credits that will allow retailers to lower prices and increase jobs across the board.

- Free and open trade initiatives. This must provide favorable circumstances for different retailers to let them provide the most innovative products and services to their customers and be competitive with foreign imports.

Each of theseissues would allow retail merchants to make more profits, provide the products that they have an expertise in, and would lead to job expansion and job growth.

SENIORS

Despite President Obama's victory over republican candidate John McCain in 2008, the current commander-in-chief now frequently finds himself at odds with one of the largest voting parties in the nation, the seniors. In a 2008 news article, "Analysis of White Seniors and the 2008 Election," it states: " . . . Obama is at odds with a majority of white seniors. . . . performance among seniors (age 65 and over) provided one of the few low points of the election when exit polls showed that President Obama lost to John McCain among seniors 45 to 53 percent." In 2008, the senior voters feared President Obama, because of the undeniable change he would bring, they remained "skeptical about whose side President Obama was on . . . and were specifically concerned about his level of experience". These feelings in particular lurked among white senior men and seniors without a college degree for "the same reasons that drew millions of supporters to President Obama—his unusual background, his quick rise to power, and his message of change" ("Analysis").

Change is inevitable and America's history is a constant testimony to that, but seniors traditionally fear change more than younger voters. They are particularly worried about their savings, taxes, changes in tax laws, and perceived threats to social security and their pensions. They need to be assured that they will be taken care of and that change is always going to happen and that it can be beneficial.

An article, from Lohuizen, in 1775, change first occurred in Lexington and Concord when a group of rebels fought to liberate themselves from the British monarchy. Again change happened in 1863 with President Lincoln's passing of the Emancipation Proclamation. In 1945, Oppenheimer's weapon changed the face of warfare as his bombs landed on Hiroshima and Nagasaki. In 1969, the world changed when the first man walked on the moon. And again, America changed dramatically in 2008 when the nation nominated the first black man to run for President. That he won was a tremendous surprise to many seniors who were alive when Black people were not even allowed to vote.

Change is inevitable. After four years into his term, President Obama has gained at least some support, or sympathy from some of the senior voters. One letter from the Resurgent Republic shows more favorable and sympathetic feelings for the President. It said, " . . . Obama Independents like the President and are hesitant to solely blame him for the economy. Their affinity is more due to personal characteristics rather than policy alignment. In fact, when asked to identify President Obama's policies they liked most, these voters tended to say President Obama inherited major problems and then shift the conversation toward his personal favorability, using words like "sincere," "smart," and "compassionate." Their blame was more directed at Washington and what they perceived as the dysfunctional nature of Congress" (Lohuizen, 2012).

Based on his actions and the fact that the economy is slowly recovery, it appears that after four years time, at least some of the senior voters are beginning to warm up to the idea of President Obama staying for another term in office. With the 2012 presidential election getting closer, it seems that many senior Americans are facing reality: change can be good.

STOCK MARKET

As reported by Elliott Wave International, since President Obama took office in January 2009, the United States Stock market and the Dow Jones Industrial Average has risen 60 percent. In his first three years of office, blue chip companies surged more than 50 percent and the overall rate of return for those who left their money invested was more than 10%. This was one of the best returns of profits for the consumer during the past 20 years. Despite the impression of the business community and the investors that President Obama is anti-business, all markets soared the first three years he was in office. Of course, there is no direct correlation of the rising or falling stock prices to that of the President's action, but one thing is clear, the social behavior of the nation may have contributed to the cause and effect of the changes in the stock market.

For those who study waves and cycles of finances, the problems that occurred in 2005 were not unexpected, but a normal occurrence of bounces or major pullback from the major stocks. Nevertheless, the rise of the stock market occurred during the term of President Obama and helped to improve a segment of the economy for all concerned. This is similar to Clinton era where the rally or run up came in after 1990 recession.

In agreement with Washington Post, in 2009, the stock market bottomed out after the 2008 financial crisis. In 2011, uncertainties in politics once again influenced the performance of DJIA as debt-ceiling debates and the credit downgrade resulted in a one-day 500 point-drop in the market. Massive sell-off into the last quarter of 2011 caused a downward pressure for the stock prices and the administration. As of this writing, the stock market is highly volatile, but it continues to slowly improve. There is no proof, but the market may heavily correct or move in a larger consolidation just before the presidential elections. On the other hand, there are indications that one last major rally is expected barring any fundamental reasons from Europe and the United States. If this happens, this will favor President Obama in his bid for his second term because the market will view this as the final trigger to ending the struggling U.S. economic growth. No matter what happens during this election year, there was a positive growth in the United State stock market during the President's first term. Those financial experts who study the waves and cycles of the market are unanimous that this is a strong indication that the worst of the recession is over and better days are coming soon.

TECHNOLOGY

If you were a teacher in high school or college today, one of your biggest discipline issues would be to keep your students from texting or looking at the internet when they were supposed to be listening to the instructor or taking notes. For these students, use of the cell phone, the internet, or listening to music on an instrument that will fit in their hand is a way of life. So are the terms facebook, tweeting, texting, and all of the other forms of social media that they use every day. This often sets them apart from their grandparents and often puts them at odds with their parents. Much more has changed in the world of technology during President Obama's first term in office as well. The rise of some forms of technology and the demise of some other forms, such as the camera that uses film has significantly influenced the profits of individuals, companies, and stock holders.

For example, the established internet distributors such as: Netflix, Hulu, You Tube, and iTunes have cultivated the digital side of the movie distribution. Streaming movies is projected to increase in revenue 20% from 2008 to 2013 while DVD and Blu-ray sales are projected to decrease by 80% during the same period. These changes in the trends in distribution channels will enable consumers to cut their cable subscriptions altogether, and will change the value of cable companies. It will also inject competition into subscription and on-demand viewing markets where online television distributors have low costs of entry, unlike cable or satellite operators, and can pose a competitive threat in markets where incumbent MVPDs have monopoly positions. It will enable film makers to bypass MVPDs and go directly to consumers, which can bring in more revenue thereby increasing net profit.

Digital platforms such as internet ready television, cell phones, and tablets are quickly evolving and so, too, are the internet capabilities such as the ever increasing bandwidth. All of these are making movie streaming the growing trend and changing the face of the movie industry. President Obama's approach does not advocate panic in the face of the uncertainty and threats brought about by far-reaching changes in technology, but rather encourages all entrepreneurs to keep working for their dream ideas.

While these newer forms of technology are competing for market share, the film industry has been unable to dictate the terms by which its products are distributed, or even to come up with alternative uses of technology that would enable its profits and returns to increase. Even a company as successful as Netflix has shown itself to be as much at the mercy of these trends as in control of them.

Thus, the companies whose stock was at the top four years ago could be slipping rapidly and the stock of companies less than a few years old could be climbing upward. The President has little control over this rapidly expanding and changing industry, but his advisors are kept busy trying to make certain that confidentiality, personal business laws, hacking, and circumvention of copyright laws are maintained and/or controlled. This requires new types of surveillance on the part of law enforcement agencies, and that Congress be kept abreast of the possibilities of patent and other infractions of the law be recognized, updated, and/or preserved. Often this requires new legislation to cover issues that were not even thought of ten years ago.

CONCLUSION

Have you learned something about the many ways that President Obama has worked to improve the economic condition of the country while reading this short book? I hope so! As a doctoral student, I have been studying these issues with more intensity than the average American. For this reason I felt that my knowledge would be of interest to many young and working Americans who don't have the time or the interest to study each of the issues. I wanted people to find in one place an overview of the successes of President Obama in his first term of office and seriously consider supporting him in 2012 if the facts warrant it. That's the purpose of this book.

As a lay-woman, I am not an expert in any of the subjects in this book, but I have tried to use my studies and experience to be impartial and look at both sides of the issues. It was my goal to show in what areas President Obama was doing a good job and was making progress toward his promises of change. I also tried to include those areas that the President has said repeatedly were critical to the health and prosperity of the United States where little, if any, progress has been made. Finally, I attempted to include some areas, such as technology, where facts and trends are changing so fast that it is hard for anyone to keep up with the new information or fully understand what it takes to protect the privacy of Americans. I thought if the readers of the book would listen to the information I have gathered through reading and studying, they might be more positive in their thoughts about the last four years.

Former President Bill Clinton once said, "Being a President is like running a cemetery; you've got a lot of people under you . . . and nobody's listening." I am sure that President Obama must feel this same way many times when he tries to explain to Congress and the nation the laws and programs he wants to enact. They may "hear" what he is saying, but most are not giving the ideas their undivided attention because they are like the rest of us—we hear what we want to hear, or we hear what we think we hear, not what the other person is actually trying to communicate.

Most of the concepts that President Obama is presenting as solutions to America's problems are worthwhile listening to and would be so beneficial to the nation if he could get them enacted. A good example are the three programs he has put forth to help struggling home owners save their "underwater" homes. If the banks and other financial institutions had only taken the time to listen and understand the programs, they might have been willing and able to put the ideas into action. Instead, it appears that they had their minds made up before they heard the whole story. The problem with this attitude is that there was nothing the President could do or say that would change the firmly held convictions of those institutions and the people who own and manage them. As a result, millions of American families lost their homes needlessly.

I am trusting that the readers of this book will open their minds to the perspectives I have presented and will have a deeper understanding of what the President is trying to do. I fervently hope that some of the readers who may have fostered preconceived prejudices about the President's job will review what he did during the first term and accept this new information with open minds. I urge you, the reader, to be a good listener to what the President has to say in his campaigning for a second term. I am confident that you will be pleased, as I am, by what he tells you he is going to do next.

REFERENCES

Almansour, M., Gaddi, E., Mendoza, S., Rostami, M., Rubio, A., & Zanjani,F. (2011).
Movie Distribution Assessment. Retrieved on July 26, 2012. Pepperdine University School of Education and Psychology, West Los Angeles Cohort.

Amadeo, K. (2012). Government Bailout of Ford GM Chrysler and the Auto Industry. Retrieved on May 30, 2012 fromwww.useconomy. about.com/ad/criticalissues/a/auto_bailout.htm

Arvai, E. (2011). Obama Proposes $100 per flight Tax on Business Turbine Aircraft.
Retrieved on June 5, 2012 from www.airinsight.com/ . . . /obama-proposes-100-per- flight-tax-on-business-tur . . .

Barnes, R. (2012). Supreme Court upholds Obama's health –care law. Retrieved on May 30, 2012 from www.washingtonpost.com/ . . . supreme-court . . . ,health-care . . . /gJOAarR . . .

Boaz, D. (2012). President Obama and the Youth Vote. Retrieved on June 20, 2012 from: www.hufingtonpost.com/ . . . boaz/obama-youth-vote-2012-election_b . . .

Boaz, D. (2012). President Obama and the Youth Vote. Retrieved on July 3, 2012 from http://www.huffingtonpost.com/david-boaz/obama-youth-vote-2012-election_b_1562775.html

Bottemiller, H. (2012). Food Industry Tells Obama Administration: No Food Safety Fees.
Retrieved on July 1, 2012 from http://www.foodsafetynews.com/ 2012/01/food- industry-tells-obama-administration-no-food-safety-fees/

Bottemiller, H. (2012). 8—Food Safety News. Retrieved on July 24, 2012 from: http://www.foodsafetynews.com/contributors/helena-bottemiller/

Burns, S. (2012). Ranks of Working Poor Growing Under Obama – the Last Chance. Retrieved on July 20, 2012 from www.thelastchanceoffreedom.blogspot.com/ . . . /ranks-of-working-poor-gro . . .

Chopra, A. (2011). Startup America: A Campaign To Celebrate, Inspire, And Accelerate Entrepreneurship. Retrieved on June 30, 2012 from: Techcrunch.com/ . . . /startup-america-a-campaign-to-celebrate-inspire-a . . .

Crutsinger, M. (2012). Unemployment could stay high as US economy slows. Retrieved on May 29, 2012 from www.boston.com/ . . . / us_economic_growth_slowed_to_15_pct_rate_i..
www.boston.com/ . . . /us_economic_growth_slowed_to_15_pct_rate _i . . .

Drehle, D., V. (2008). Obama's Youth Vote Triumph. Retrieved on June 4, 2012 from http://www.time.com/time/politics/article/0,8599, 1700525,00.html

Elliott Wave International: Waves and Cylces, 2012. www.elliottwave.com/

Falcone, J.P. (2008). Netflix watch now: missing too much popular content. Retrieved on from November 2, 2011 from news.cnet.com/8301-17938_105-9940529-1.html.

Fernholz, T. (2009). Make This Speech in Prime Time. Retrieved on July 22, 2012 from www.prospect.org/article/make-speech-prime-time

Forssell, A. (2010). Hulu – about. Retrieved on November 4, 2011 from http://www.hulu.com/about/executive.

Fulkner, L. (2011). Netflix price hike – not such a great idea? Retrieved on November 4, 2011 from https://secure.hosting.vt.edu/www.marketing.pamplin . . . /blog.php . . .

Gill, K. (2009). President Barack Obama' State of the Union Address. Retrieved on from www.uspolitics.about.com/od/speeches/a/24feb2009_obama.htm

Hinds, S. (2012). Obama's "Fair Share" Crusade Continues Via Aviation Fees. Retrieved on July 6,2012 from http://thecollegeconservative.com/2012/03/20/obamas-fair-share-cru . . .

Homeless Veteran Advocacy: President Obama, Michelle Obama Receive Highest Award in Homeless Veteran Advocay (2012). Retrieved on June 15, 2012 from http://www.huffingtonpost.com/2012/04/27/veteran-homelessness-barack-obama_n_1459433.html

Huang, E., Sisk, J., Kirk, T., Coryell, G., & Stewart, J. (2004). Searching for an ideal live video streaming technology. Retrieved June 15, 2012 from www.iupui.edu/~nmstream/live/introduction.php.

Huffington Post: Obama Budget Proposal: Cuts To Target Working Poor, Middle Class, & Students (2011). Retrieved on June 15, 2012 from http://www.huffingtonpost.com/2011/02/13/obama-budget-proposal-cut_n_822689.html

Huffington Post: Obama Speech: State of the Union Address . . . -Huffington Post. Retrieved on June 18, 2012 from www.huffingtonpost.com/ . . . obama-speech-state-of-the-union_n_12 . . .

Huffington Post: Print Media, 2012. www.huffingtonpost.com/

Inaugural Address: President Barack Obama's Inaugural Address (2009). The White House Retrieved on July 15, 2012 from: www.whitehouse. gov/blog/inaugural-address

Jackson, J., & Nolen, J. (2010). Health Care Reform Bill Summary: A Look At What's in the Bill. Retrieved on June 25, 2012 from http:// www.cbsnews.com/8301-503544_162-20000846-503544.html

Jacobson, L. (2012). A scorecard on the economy under Barack Obama Retrieved on June 5, 2012 from http://www.politifact.com/truth-o-meter/article/2012/jun/01/scorecar . . .

Jobs and the Economy: President Obama's Record –Barack Obama. Retrieved on July 9, 2012 from www.barackobama.com/record/

Jones, N. (2012). Unfair or Necessary? Obama's Proposed Per-Flight Tax on Private . . . Retrieved on July 22, 2012 from: waynefarley.com/ . . . /unfair-or-necessary-obama's- proposed-per—flight . . .

Keeter, S.; Horowitz, J. & Tyson, A. (2008).Young Voters in the 2008 Election. Retrieved June 7, 2012 from www.pewresearch.org/ pubs/1031/young-voters-in-the-2008-election

Klein, J. (2010). Why We're Failing Our Schools. Retrieved on June 30, 2012 from http://www.time.com/time/magazine/article/0,9171, 1957470,00.html

Kreiter, M. (2012). Jobs: The number of baby boomers retiring is holding down the Unemployment rate. Retrieved on July 1, 2012 from: www. upi.com

Kumral, D. (2008). Streaming video technology and its advantages by viewing and recording streaming videos live and on demand. Retrieved November 10, 2011 from www.savevid.com/the-advantages-of-streaming-video-technology.html.

Linsay, E. (2011). The Resurgence of the American Automotive Industry. Retrieved on June 2, 2012 from www.whitehouse.gov/ . . . /2011 . . . / resurgence-american-automotive-in . . .

Lohuizen, J.V., & Gillespie, E. (2012). The Economy and Health Care are Determining Factors for Seniors in 2012. Retrieved on June 10, 2012 from http://www.tampabay.com/blogs/ the-buzz-florida-politics/ sites/tampabay.com.blogs.the-buzz-florida-politics/files/rrsenior voterfocusgroupsmemo.pdf

Malveaux, J. (2012). Jobs Numbers Could Affect Obama's Ability to Keep His Job. Retrieved on July 17, 2012 from: http://washingtoninformer. com/index.php/financial-literacy/item/1112 . . .

Mantell, R. &Coombes, A., (2008) Emergency Economic Stabilization Act of 2008. Retrieved on June22, 2012 from www.articles.marketwatch. com/2008 . . . /30706115_1_bailout-bill-draft-bill- . . .

McClellan, J. (2012). Restaurants opposed to Obama's health care law ruling. Retrieved on June 25, 2012 from: www.azcentral.com/ . . . / dining/articles/ . . . 20120628restaurants-oppose . . .

Nagourney, A. (2008). Obama Wins Election; McCain Loses as Bush Legacy Is Rejected. Retrieved on July 4, 2012 from http://www.nytimes. com/2008/11/05/us/politics/05campaign.html?_r=1&pagewanted=all

National Alliance to End Homelessness: The 2012 National Conference on Ending Homelessness (2012) Retrieved on June 5, 2012 from www. endhomelessness.org/content/general/list/

Newsmax: Ranks of Working Poor Growing Under Obama (2012). Retrieved on June 2, 2012 from: http://www.newsmax.com/Newsfront/ obama-working-poor-growing/2012/04/06/id/435122

New York Grub Street: The Restaurant Industry Is Not Psyched About . . . —Grub Street Retrieved on July 6, 2012 from: newyork.grubstreet. com/ . . . /the-restaurant-industry-on-obamacare.ht . . .

No Child Left Behind Act: Archived: Executive Summary of the No Child Left Behind Act of 2001. Retrieved on July 15, 2012 from: www. ed.gov/nclb/overview/intro/execsumm.html

Presidential Candidates: Obama Position on Education (2012). Retrieved on May 30, 2012 from http://2012.presidential-candidates.org/ Obama/Education-issue.php

Preston, J. & Cushman, J.H. (2012).U.S. to Stop Deporting Some Immigrants. Retrieved on May 31, 2012 from www.nytimes.com/ . . . /us-to-stop-deporting-some-illegal-im . . .

Pugh, T. (2010). Obama vows to end homelessness in 10 years. Retrieved on July 2, 2012 from http://www.mcclatchydc.com/2010/06/22/96322/obama-administration-vows-to-end.html

Ranks of Working Poor Growing Under Obama (2012) Retrieved on July 12, 2012 from www.newsmax.com/Newsfront/obama-working-poor . . . / id/435122

Resmovits, J. H. (2012). No Child Left Behind Waivers Granted to 33 U.S. States. Retrieved on June 22, 2012 from: www.huffingtonpost.com/ . . . /no-child-left-behind-waiver_n . . .

Roman, N. (2012). Homeless in America: 636,017; Homeless veterans: 67,495 Retrieved on on June 30, 2012 from www.hehill.com/ . . . /208085-homeless-in-america-636017-homeless-vetera . . .

Rosenberg, M. (2009).The Population Baby Boom of 1946-1964 in the United States. Retrieved on July 15, 2012from: www.geography.about.com/od/populationgeography/a/babyboom.htm

Shearman, J. C.(2012). National Retail Federation – NRF Urges Obama to Address Retail. Retrieved on July 6, 2012 from: www.nrf.com/modules.php?name=News&op=viewlive&sp_id . . .

Shelasky, A. (2012). Grub Street: New York Magazine's Food . . . Retrieved on July 5, 2012 from: newyork.grubstreet.com/2012/06/28/

Shepherd, J. (2010). World education rankings: which country does best at reading, maths, and science? Retrieved on June 10, 2012 from http://www.guardian.co.uk/news/datablog/   2010/dec/07/world-education-rankings-maths-science-reading

State of Homelessness: Chapter One –Homelessness Counts (2012). Retrieved on July 2, 2012 from http://www.endhomelessness.org/content/article/detail/4362

Stiglitz, J. (2012). The Economic Consequences of Mr. Bush. Retrieved on June 1, 2012 from: www.vanityfair.com/politics/features/2007/12/bush200712

United States: Organization for Economic Co-operation and Development (2012). Retrieved on June 1, 2012 from: www.oecd.org/unitedstates/

Washington DC: About Washington DC (2012) Retrieved on May 25, 2012 from: www.washington.org/about-washington-dc/

Washington Post: Stock Market Behavior, 2012 www.washingtonpost.com/

www.ingramcontent.com/pod-product-compliance
Lightning Source LLC
Chambersburg PA
CBHW020358290526
45785CB00005B/2349